'THE ULTIMATE CAMP STATEMENT: IT'S GOOD BECAUSE IT'S AWFUL.'

SUSAN SONTAG
Born 1933, New York, USA
Died 2004, New York, USA

'Notes on "Camp"' and 'One Culture and the New Sensibility'
are both taken from *Against Interpretation and Other Essays*,
first published in 1966.

SUSAN SONTAG

Notes on 'Camp'

PENGUIN BOOKS

PENGUIN CLASSICS

UK | USA | Canada | Ireland | Australia
India | New Zealand | South Africa

Penguin Books is part of the Penguin Random House group
of companies whose addresses can be found at
global.penguinrandomhouse.com.

Penguin
Random House
UK

This selection first published 2018
025

Set in 12/15 pt Dante MT Std
Typeset by Jouve (UK), Milton Keynes
Printed and bound in Great Britain by Clays Ltd, Elcograf S.p.A.

ISBN: 978-0-241-33970-1

www.greenpenguin.co.uk

MIX
Paper | Supporting
responsible forestry
FSC® C018072

Penguin Random House is committed to a
sustainable future for our business, our readers
and our planet. This book is made from Forest
Stewardship Council® certified paper.

Contents

Notes on 'Camp'

Many things in the world have not been named; and many things, even if they have been named, have never been described. One of these is the sensibility – unmistakably modern, a variant of sophistication but hardly identical with it – that goes by the cult name of 'Camp.'

A sensibility (as distinct from an idea) is one of the hardest things to talk about; but there are special reasons why Camp, in particular, has never been discussed. It is not a natural mode of sensibility, if there be any such. Indeed the essence of Camp is its love of the unnatural: of artifice and exaggeration. And Camp is esoteric – something of a private code, a badge of identity even, among small urban cliques. Apart from a lazy two-page sketch in Christopher Isherwood's novel *The World in the Evening* (1954), it has hardly broken into print. To talk about Camp is therefore to betray it. If the betrayal can be defended, it will be for the edification it provides, or the dignity of the conflict it resolves. For myself, I plead the goal of self-edification, and the goad of a sharp conflict in my own sensibility. I am strongly drawn to Camp, and almost as strongly offended by it. That is why I want to talk about it, and why I can. For no one who wholeheartedly shares in a given sensibility can analyze it; he can only, whatever his intention, exhibit it. To name a sensibility, to draw its contours and to recount its history, requires a deep sympathy modified by revulsion.

Though I am speaking about sensibility only – and about a sensibility that, among other things, converts the serious into the frivolous – these are grave matters. Most people think of sensibility or taste as the realm of purely subjective preferences, those mysterious attractions, mainly sensual, that have not been brought under the sovereignty of reason. They *allow* that considerations of taste play a part in their reactions to people and to works of art. But this attitude is naïve. And even worse. To patronize the faculty of taste is to patronize oneself. For taste governs every free – as opposed to rote – human response. Nothing is more decisive. There is taste in people, visual taste, taste in emotion – and there is taste in acts, taste in morality. Intelligence, as well, is really a kind of taste: taste in ideas. (One of the facts to be reckoned with is that taste tends to develop very unevenly. It's rare that the same person has good visual taste *and* good taste in people *and* taste in ideas.)

Taste has no system and no proofs. But there is something like a logic of taste: the consistent sensibility which underlies and gives rise to a certain taste. A sensibility is almost, but not quite, ineffable. Any sensibility which can be crammed into the mold of a system, or handled with the rough tools of proof, is no longer a sensibility at all. It has hardened into an idea . . .

To snare a sensibility in words, especially one that is alive and powerful,* one must be tentative and

---

* The sensibility of an era is not only its most decisive, but also its most perishable, aspect. One may capture the ideas (intellectual history) and the behavior (social history) of an epoch without ever touching upon the sensibility or taste which informed those ideas, that behavior. Rare are those historical studies – like Huizinga on the late Middle Ages, Febvre on 16th century

3

nimble. The form of jottings, rather than an essay (with its claim to a linear, consecutive argument), seemed more appropriate for getting down something of this particular fugitive sensibility. It's embarrassing to be solemn and treatise-like about Camp. One runs the risk of having, oneself, produced a very inferior piece of Camp.

These notes are for Oscar Wilde.

'One should either be a work of art, or wear a work of art.'

– Phrases & Philosophies for the
Use of the Young

1. To start very generally: Camp is a certain mode of aestheticism. It is one way of seeing the world as an aesthetic phenomenon. That way, the way of Camp, is not in terms of beauty, but in terms of the degree of artifice, of stylization.

2. To emphasize style is to slight content, or to introduce an attitude which is neutral with respect to

France – which do tell us something about the sensibility of the period.

content. It goes without saying that the Camp sensibility is disengaged, depoliticized – or at least apolitical.

3. Not only is there a Camp vision, a Camp way of looking at things, Camp is as well a quality discoverable in objects and the behavior of persons. There are 'campy' movies, clothes, furniture, popular songs, novels, people, buildings . . . This distinction is important. True, the Camp eye has the power to transform experience. But not everything can be seen as Camp. It's not *all* in the eye of the beholder.

4. Random examples of items which are part of the canon of Camp:

> *Zuleika Dobson*
> Tiffany lamps
> Scopitone films
> The Brown Derby restaurant on Sunset
>   Boulevard in LA
> *The Enquirer*, headlines and stories
> Aubrey Beardsley drawings
> *Swan Lake*
> Bellini's operas

Visconti's direction of *Salome* and *'Tis Pity She's a Whore*

Certain turn-of-the-century picture postcards

Schoedsack's *King Kong*

The Cuban pop singer La Lupe

Lynn Ward's novel in woodcuts, *God's Man*

The old Flash Gordon comics

Women's clothes of the twenties (feather boas, fringed and beaded dresses, etc.)

The novels of Ronald Firbank and Ivy Compton-Burnett

Stag movies seen without lust

5. Camp taste has an affinity for certain arts rather than others. Clothes, furniture, all the elements of visual décor, for instance, make up a large part of Camp. For Camp art is often decorative art, emphasizing texture, sensuous surface and style at the expense of content. Concert music, though, because it is contentless, is rarely Camp. It offers no opportunity, say, for a contrast between silly or extravagant content and rich form . . . Sometimes whole art forms become saturated with Camp. Classical ballet, opera, movies have seemed so for a long time. In the

last two years, popular music (post rock'n'roll, what the French call *yé yé*) has been annexed. And movie criticism (like lists of 'The 10 Best Bad Movies I Have Seen') is probably the greatest popularizer of Camp taste today, because most people still go to the movies in a high-spirited and unpretentious way.

6. There is a sense in which it is correct to say: 'It's too good to be Camp.' Or 'too important', not marginal enough. (More on this later.) Thus, the personality and many of the works of Jean Cocteau are Camp, but not those of André Gide; the operas of Richard Strauss, but not those of Wagner; concoctions of Tin Pan Alley and Liverpool, but not jazz. Many examples of Camp are things which, from a 'serious' point of view, are either bad art or kitsch. Not all, though. Not only is Camp not necessarily bad art, but some art which can be approached as Camp (example: the major films of Louis Feuillade) merits the most serious admiration and study.

'The more we study Art, the less we care for Nature.'

– *The Decay of Lying*

7. All Camp objects, and persons, contain a large element of artifice. Nothing in nature can be campy . . . Rural Camp is still man-made, and most campy objects are urban. (Yet, they often have a serenity – or a naïveté – which is the equivalent of pastoral. A great deal of Camp suggests Empson's phrase, 'urban pastoral'.)

8. Camp is a vision of the world in terms of style – but a particular kind of style. It is the love of the exaggerated, the 'off', of things-being-what-they-are-not. The best example is in Art Nouveau, the most typical and fully developed Camp style. Art Nouveau objects, typically, convert one thing into something else: the lighting fixtures in the form of flowering plants, the living room which is really a grotto. A remarkable example: the Paris Métro entrances designed by Hector Guimard in the late 1890s in the shape of cast-iron orchid stalks.

9. As a taste in persons, Camp responds particularly to the markedly attenuated and to the strongly exaggerated. The androgyne is certainly one of the great images of Camp sensibility. Examples: the swooning, slim, sinuous figures of pre-Raphaelite painting and poetry; the thin, flowing, sexless bodies

in Art Nouveau prints and posters, presented in relief on lamps and ashtrays; the haunting androgynous vacancy behind the perfect beauty of Greta Garbo. Here, Camp taste draws on a mostly unacknowledged truth of taste: the most refined form of sexual attractiveness (as well as the most refined form of sexual pleasure) consists in going against the grain of one's sex. What is most beautiful in virile men is something feminine; what is most beautiful in feminine women is something masculine . . . Allied to the Camp taste for the androgynous is something that seems quite different but isn't: a relish for the exaggeration of sexual characteristics and personality mannerisms. For obvious reasons, the best examples that can be cited are movie stars. The corny flamboyant femaleness of Jayne Mansfield, Gina Lollobrigida, Jane Russell, Virginia Mayo; the exaggerated he-man-ness of Steve Reeves, Victor Mature. The great stylists of temperament and mannerism, such as Bette Davis, Barbara Stanwyck, Tallulah Bankhead, Edwige Feuillère.

10. Camp sees everything in quotation marks. It's not a lamp, but a 'lamp'; not a woman, but a 'woman'. To perceive Camp in objects and persons is to understand Being-as-Playing-a-Role. It is the farthest

extension, in sensibility, of the metaphor of life as theater.

11. Camp is the triumph of the epicene style. (The convertibility of 'man' and 'woman', 'person' and 'thing'.) But all style, that is, artifice, is, ultimately, epicene. Life is not stylish. Neither is nature.

12. The question isn't, 'Why travesty, impersonation, theatricality?' The question is, rather, 'When does travesty, impersonation, theatricality acquire the special flavor of Camp?' Why is the atmosphere of Shakespeare's comedies (*As You Like It*, etc.) not epicene, while that of *Der Rosenkavalier* is?

13. The dividing line seems to fall in the 18th century; there the origins of Camp taste are to be found (Gothic novels, chinoiserie, caricature, artificial ruins, and so forth.) But the relation to nature was quite different then. In the 18th century, people of taste either patronized nature (Strawberry Hill) or attempted to remake it into something artificial (Versailles). They also indefatigably patronized the past. Today's Camp taste effaces nature, or else contradicts it outright. And the relation of Camp taste to the past is extremely sentimental.

14. A pocket history of Camp might, of course, begin farther back – with the mannerist artists like Pontormo, Rosso and Caravaggio, or the extraordinarily theatrical painting of Georges de La Tour, or Euphuism (Lyly, etc.) in literature. Still, the soundest starting point seems to be the late 17th and early 18th century, because of that period's extraordinary feeling for artifice, for surface, for symmetry; its taste for the picturesque and the thrilling, its elegant conventions for representing instant feeling and the total presence of character – the epigram and the rhymed couplet (in words), the flourish (in gesture and in music). The late 17th and early 18th century is the great period of Camp: Pope, Congreve, Walpole, etc., but not Swift; *les précieux* in France; the rococo churches of Munich; Pergolesi. Somewhat later: much of Mozart. But in the 19th century, what had been distributed throughout all of high culture now becomes a special taste; it takes on overtones of the acute, the esoteric, the perverse. Confining the story to England alone, we see Camp continuing wanly through 19th-century aestheticism (Burne-Jones, Pater, Ruskin, Tennyson), emerging full-blown with

the Art Nouveau movement in the visual and decorative arts, and finding its conscious ideologists in
such 'wits' as Wilde and Firbank.

15. Of course, to say all these things are Camp is
not to argue they are simply that. A full analysis of
Art Nouveau, for instance, would scarcely equate it
with Camp. But such an analysis cannot ignore what
in Art Nouveau allows it to be experienced as Camp.
Art Nouveau is full of 'content', even of a political-
moral sort; it was a revolutionary movement in the
arts, spurred on by a utopian vision (somewhere
between William Morris and the Bauhaus group) of
an organic politics and taste. Yet there is also a feature
of the Art Nouveau objects which suggests a disengaged, unserious, 'aesthete's' vision. This tells us
something important about Art Nouveau – and about
what the lens of Camp, which blocks out content, is.

16. Thus, the Camp sensibility is one that is alive
to a double sense in which some things can be taken.
But this is not the familiar split-level construction of
a literal meaning, on the one hand, and a symbolic
meaning, on the other. It is the difference, rather,
between the thing as meaning something, anything,
and the thing as pure artifice.

17. This comes out clearly in the vulgar use of the word Camp as a verb, 'to camp', something that people do. To camp is a mode of seduction – one which employs flamboyant mannerisms susceptible of a double interpretation: gestures full of duplicity, with a witty meaning for cognoscenti and another, more impersonal, for outsiders. Equally and by extension, when the word becomes a noun, when a person or a thing is 'a camp', a duplicity is involved. Behind the 'straight' public sense in which something can be taken, one has found a private zany experience of the thing.

> 'To be natural is such a very difficult pose to keep up.'
>
> – *An Ideal Husband*

18. One must distinguish between naïve and deliberate Camp. Pure Camp is always naïve. Camp which knows itself to be Camp ('camping') is usually less satisfying.

19. The pure examples of Camp are unintentional; they are dead serious. The Art Nouveau craftsman who makes a lamp with a snake coiled around it is

13

not kidding, nor is he trying to be charming. He is saying, in all earnestness: Voilà! the Orient! Genuine Camp – for instance, the numbers devised for the Warner Brothers musicals of the early thirties (*42nd Street*; *The Golddiggers of 1933*; . . . *of 1935*; . . . *of 1937*; etc.) by Busby Berkeley – does not *mean* to be funny. Camping – say, the plays of Noël Coward – does. It seems unlikely that much of the traditional opera repertoire could be such satisfying Camp if the melodramatic absurdities of most opera plots had not been taken seriously by their composers. One doesn't need to know the artist's private intentions. The work tells all. (Compare a typical 19th century opera with Samuel Barber's *Vanessa*, a piece of manufactured, calculated Camp, and the difference is clear.)

20. Probably, intending to be campy is always harmful. The perfection of *Trouble in Paradise* and *The Maltese Falcon*, among the greatest Camp movies ever made, comes from the effortless smooth way in which tone is maintained. This is not so with such famous would-be Camp films of the fifties as *All About Eve* and *Beat the Devil*. These more recent movies have their fine moments, but the first is so slick

and the second so hysterical; they want so badly to be campy that they're continually losing the beat . . . Perhaps, though, it is not so much a question of the unintended effect versus the conscious intention, as of the delicate relation between parody and self-parody in Camp. The films of Hitchcock are a showcase for this problem. When self-parody lacks ebullience but instead reveals (even sporadically) a contempt for one's themes and one's materials – as in *To Catch a Thief, Rear Window, North by Northwest* – the results are forced and heavy-handed, rarely Camp. Successful Camp – a movie like Carné's *Drôle de Drame*; the film performances of Mae West and Edward Everett Horton; portions of the Goon Show – even when it reveals self-parody, reeks of self-love.

21. So, again, Camp rests on innocence. That means Camp discloses innocence, but also, when it can, corrupts it. Objects, being objects, don't change when they are singled out by the Camp vision. Persons, however, respond to their audiences. Persons begin 'camping': Mae West, Bea Lillie, La Lupe, Tallulah Bankhead in *Lifeboat*, Bette Davis in *All About*

Eve. (Persons can even be induced to camp without their knowing it. Consider the way Fellini got Anita Ekberg to parody herself in *La Dolce Vita*.)

22. Considered a little less strictly, Camp is either completely naïve or else wholly conscious (when one plays at being campy). An example of the latter: Wilde's epigrams themselves.

> 'It's absurd to divide people into good and bad. People are either charming or tedious.'
>
> – *Lady Windermere's Fan*

23. In naïve, or pure, Camp, the essential element is seriousness, a seriousness that fails. Of course, not all seriousness that fails can be redeemed as Camp. Only that which has the proper mixture of the exaggerated, the fantastic, the passionate and the naïve.

24. When something is just bad (rather than Camp), it's often because it is too mediocre in its ambition. The artist hasn't attempted to do anything really outlandish. ('It's too much', 'It's too fantastic', 'It's not to be believed,' are standard phrases of Camp enthusiasm.)

25. The hallmark of Camp is the spirit of extravagance. Camp is a woman walking around in a dress

made of three million feathers. Camp is the paintings of Carlo Crivelli, with their real jewels and
trompe-l'oeil insects and cracks in the masonry. Camp
is the outrageous aestheticism of Sternberg's six
American movies with Dietrich, all six, but especially
the last, *The Devil Is a Woman* . . . In Camp there is
often something *démesuré* in the quality of the ambition, not only in the style of the work itself. Gaudí's
lurid and beautiful buildings in Barcelona are Camp
not only because of their style but because they
reveal – most notably in the Cathedral of the Sagrada
Família – the ambition on the part of one man to do
what it takes a generation, a whole culture to
accomplish.

26. Camp is art that proposes itself seriously, but
cannot be taken altogether seriously because it is
'too much'. *Titus Andronicus* and *Strange Interlude* are
almost Camp, or could be played as Camp. The public manner and rhetoric of de Gaulle, often, are pure
Camp.

27. A work can come close to Camp, but not
make it, because it succeeds. Eisenstein's films are
seldom Camp because, despite all exaggeration, they
do succeed (dramatically) without surplus. If they

were a little more 'off', they could be great Camp –
particularly *Ivan the Terrible I & II*. The same for
Blake's drawings and paintings, weird and mannered
as they are. They aren't Camp; though Art Nouveau,
influenced by Blake, is.

What is extravagant in an inconsistent or an
unpassionate way is not Camp. Neither can anything
be Camp that does not seem to spring from an irre-
pressible, a virtually uncontrolled sensibility.
Without passion, one gets pseudo-Camp – what is
merely decorative, safe, in a word, chic. On the bar-
ren edge of Camp lie a number of attractive things:
the sleek fantasies of Dalí, the haute couture preciosity of Albicocco's *The Girl with the Golden Eyes*. But
the two things – Camp and preciosity – must not be
confused.

28. Again, Camp is the attempt to do something
extraordinary. But extraordinary in the sense, often,
of being special, glamorous. (The curved line, the
extravagant gesture.) Not extraordinary merely in
the sense of effort. Ripley's Believe-It-Or-Not items
are rarely campy. These items, either natural oddities
(the two-headed rooster, the eggplant in the shape
of a cross) or else the products of immense labor

(the man who walked from here to China on his hands, the woman who engraved the New Testament on the head of a pin), lack the visual reward – the glamour, the theatricality – that marks off certain extravagances as Camp.

29. The reason a movie like *On the Beach*, books like *Winesburg, Ohio* and *For Whom the Bell Tolls* are bad to the point of being laughable, but not bad to the point of being enjoyable, is that they are too dogged and pretentious. They lack fantasy. There is Camp in such bad movies as *The Prodigal* and *Samson and Delilah*, the series of Italian color spectacles featuring the super-hero Maciste, numerous Japanese science fiction films (*Rodan*, *The Mysterians*, *The H-Man*) because, in their relative unpretentiousness and vulgarity, they are more extreme and irresponsible in their fantasy – and therefore touching and quite enjoyable.

30. Of course, the canon of Camp can change. Time has a great deal to do with it. Time may enhance what seems simply dogged or lacking in fantasy now because we are too close to it, because it resembles too closely our own everyday fantasies, the fantastic nature of which we don't perceive. We

are better able to enjoy a fantasy as fantasy when it is not our own.

31. This is why so many of the objects prized by Camp taste are old-fashioned, out-of-date, *démodé*. It's not a love of the old as such. It's simply that the process of aging or deterioration provides the necessary detachment – or arouses a necessary sympathy. When the theme is important, and contemporary, the failure of a work of art may make us indignant. Time can change that. Time liberates the work of art from moral relevance, delivering it over to the Camp sensibility . . . Another effect: time contracts the sphere of banality. (Banality is, strictly speaking, always a category of the contemporary.) What was banal can, with the passage of time, become fantastic. Many people who listen with delight to the style of Rudy Vallée revived by the English pop group, The Temperance Seven, would have been driven up the wall by Rudy Vallée in his heyday.

Thus, things are campy, not when they become old – but when we become less involved in them, and can enjoy, instead of be frustrated by, the failure of the attempt. But the effect of time is unpredictable. Maybe Method acting (James Dean, Rod

Steiger, Warren Beatty) will seem as Camp some day as Ruby Keeler's does now – or as Sarah Bernhardt's does, in the films she made at the end of her career. And maybe not.

32. Camp is the glorification of 'character.' The statement is of no importance – except, of course, to the person (Loie Fuller, Gaudí, Cecil B. De Mille, Crivelli, de Gaulle, etc.) who makes it. What the Camp eye appreciates is the unity, the force of the person. In every move the aging Martha Graham makes she's being Martha Graham, etc., etc. . . . This is clear in the case of the great serious idol of Camp taste, Greta Garbo. Garbo's incompetence (at the least, lack of depth) as an *actress* enhances her beauty. She's always herself.

33. What Camp taste responds to is 'instant character' (this is, of course, very 18th century); and, conversely, what it is not stirred by is the sense of the development of character. Character is understood as a state of continual incandescence – a person being one, very intense thing. This attitude toward character is a key element of the theatricalization of experience embodied in the Camp sensibility. And it helps account for the fact that opera and ballet are

experienced as such rich treasures of Camp, for neither of these forms can easily do justice to the complexity of human nature. Wherever there is development of character, Camp is reduced. Among operas, for example, *La Traviata* (which has some small development of character) is less campy than *Il Trovatore* (which has none).

> 'Life is too important a thing ever to talk seriously about it.'
>
> – *Vera, or The Nihilists*

34. Camp taste turns its back on the good–bad axis of ordinary aesthetic judgment. Camp doesn't reverse things. It doesn't argue that the good is bad, or the bad is good. What it does is to offer for art (and life) a different – a supplementary – set of standards.

35. Ordinarily we value a work of art because of the seriousness and dignity of what it achieves. We value it because it succeeds – in being what it is and, presumably, in fulfilling the intention that lies behind it. We assume a proper, that is to say, straightforward relation between intention and performance. By such

standards, we appraise *The Iliad*, Aristophanes' plays, *The Art of the Fugue*, *Middlemarch*, the paintings of Rembrandt, Chartres, the poetry of Donne, *The Divine Comedy*, Beethoven's quartets, and – among people – Socrates, Jesus, St Francis, Napoleon, Savonarola. In short, the pantheon of high culture: truth, beauty and seriousness.

36. But there are other creative sensibilities besides the seriousness (both tragic and comic) of high culture and of the high style of evaluating people. And one cheats oneself, as a human being, if one has respect only for the style of high culture, whatever else one may do or feel on the sly.

For instance, there is the kind of seriousness whose trademark is anguish, cruelty, derangement. Here we do accept a disparity between intention and result. I am speaking, obviously, of a style of personal existence as well as of a style in art; but the examples had best come from art. Think of Bosch, Sade, Rimbaud, Jarry, Kafka, Artaud, think of most of the important works of art of the 20th century, that is, art whose goal is not that of creating harmonies but of overstraining the medium and introducing more and more violent, and unresolvable, subject-matter. This sensibility also insists on the principle that an *oeuvre* in the old sense (again, in art, but also in life) is not possible. Only 'fragments' are possible ... Clearly, different standards apply here than to traditional high culture. Something is good not because it is achieved, but because another kind of truth about the human situation, another experience of what it is to be human – in short, another valid sensibility – is being revealed.

And third among the great creative sensibilities is Camp: the sensibility of failed seriousness, of the theatricalization of experience. Camp refuses both the harmonies of traditional seriousness, and the risks of fully identifying with extreme states of feeling.

37. The first sensibility, that of high culture, is basically moralistic. The second sensibility, that of extreme states of feeling, represented in much contemporary 'avant-garde' art, gains power by a tension between moral and aesthetic passion. The third, Camp, is wholly aesthetic.

38. Camp is the consistently aesthetic experience of the world. It incarnates a victory of 'style' over

'content', 'aesthetics' over 'morality', of irony over tragedy.

39. Camp and tragedy are antitheses. There is seriousness in Camp (seriousness in the degree of the artist's involvement) and, often, pathos. The excruciating is also one of the tonalities of Camp; it is the quality of excruciation in much of Henry James (for instance, *The Europeans*, *The Awkward Age*, *The Wings of the Dove*) that is responsible for the large element of Camp in his writings. But there is never, never tragedy.

40. Style is everything. Genet's ideas, for instance, are very Camp. Genet's statement that 'the only criterion of an act is its elegance'* is virtually inter-changeable, as a statement, with Wilde's 'in matters of great importance, the vital element is not sincerity, but style.' But what counts, finally, is the style in which ideas are held. The ideas about morality and politics in, say, *Lady Windermere's Fan* and in *Major*

* Sartre's gloss on this in *Saint Genet* is: 'Elegance is the quality of conduct which transforms the greatest amount of being into appearing.'

Barbara are Camp, but not just because of the nature of the ideas themselves. It is those ideas, held in a special playful way. The Camp ideas in *Our Lady of the Flowers* are maintained too grimly, and the writing itself is too successfully elevated and serious, for Genet's books to be Camp.

41. The whole point of Camp is to dethrone the serious. Camp is playful, anti-serious. More precisely, Camp involves a new, more complex relation to 'the serious'. One can be serious about the frivolous, frivolous about the serious.

42. One is drawn to Camp when one realizes that 'sincerity' is not enough. Sincerity can be simple philistinism, intellectual narrowness.

43. The traditional means for going beyond straight seriousness – irony, satire – seem feeble today, inadequate to the culturally oversaturated medium in which contemporary sensibility is schooled. Camp introduces a new standard: artifice as an ideal, theatricality.

44. Camp proposes a comic vision of the world. But not a bitter or polemical comedy. If tragedy is an experience of hyperinvolvement, comedy is an experience of underinvolvement, of detachment.

'I adore simple pleasures, they are the last refuge of the complex.'

– *A Woman of No Importance*

45. Detachment is the prerogative of an elite; and as the dandy is the 19th century's surrogate for the aristocrat in matters of culture, so Camp is the modern dandyism. Camp is the answer to the problem: how to be a dandy in the age of mass culture.

46. The dandy was overbred. His posture was disdain, or else *ennui*. He sought rare sensations, undefiled by mass appreciation. (Models: Des Esseintes in Huysmans' *À Rebours*, *Marius the Epicurean*, Valéry's *Monsieur Teste*.) He was dedicated to 'good taste'.

The connoisseur of Camp has found more ingenious pleasures. Not in Latin poetry and rare wines and velvet jackets, but in the coarsest, commonest pleasures, in the arts of the masses. Mere use does not defile the objects of his pleasure, since he learns to possess them in a rare way. Camp – Dandyism in the age of mass culture – makes no distinction between the unique object and the mass-produced object. Camp taste transcends the nausea of the replica.

47. Wilde himself is a transitional figure. The man who, when he first came to London, sported a velvet beret, lace shirts, velveteen knee-breeches and black silk stockings, could never depart too far in his life from the pleasures of the old-style dandy; this conservatism is reflected in *The Picture of Dorian Gray*. But many of his attitudes suggest something more modern. It was Wilde who formulated an important element of the Camp sensibility – the equivalence of all objects – when he announced his intention of 'living up' to his blue-and-white china, or declared that a door-knob could be as admirable as a painting. When he proclaimed the importance of the necktie, the boutonnière, the chair, Wilde was anticipating the democratic *esprit* of Camp.

48. The old-style dandy hated vulgarity. The new-style dandy, the lover of Camp, appreciates vulgarity. Where the dandy would be continually offended or bored, the connoisseur of Camp is continually amused, delighted. The dandy held a perfumed handkerchief to his nostrils and was liable to swoon; the connoisseur of Camp sniffs the stink and prides himself on his strong nerves.

49. It is a feat, of course. A feat goaded on, in the last analysis, by the threat of boredom. The relation between boredom and Camp taste cannot be overestimated. Camp taste is by its nature possible only in affluent societies, in societies or circles capable of experiencing the psychopathology of affluence.

> 'What is abnormal in Life stands in normal relations to Art. It is the only thing in Life that stands in normal relations to Art.'
>
> – *A Few Maxims for the Instruction of the Over-Educated*

50. Aristocracy is a position vis-à-vis culture (as well as vis-à-vis power), and the history of Camp taste is part of the history of snob taste. But since no authentic aristocrats in the old sense exist today to sponsor special tastes, who is the bearer of this taste? Answer: an improvised self-elected class, mainly homosexuals, who constitute themselves as aristocrats of taste.

51. The peculiar relation beween Camp taste and homosexuality has to be explained. While it's not

true that Camp taste is homosexual taste, there is no doubt a peculiar affinity and overlap. Not all liberals are Jews, but Jews have shown a peculiar affinity for liberal and reformist causes. So, not all homosexuals have Camp taste. But homosexuals, by and large, constitute the vanguard – and the most articulate audience – of Camp. (The analogy is not frivolously chosen. Jews and homosexuals are the outstanding creative minorities in contemporary urban culture. Creative, that is, in the truest sense: they are creators of sensibilities. The two pioneering forces of modern sensibility are Jewish moral seriousness and homosexual aestheticism and irony.)

52. The reason for the flourishing of the aristocratic posture among homosexuals also seems to parallel the Jewish case. For every sensibility is self-serving to the group that promotes it. Jewish liberalism is a gesture of self-legitimization. So is Camp taste, which definitely has something propagandistic about it. Needless to say, the propaganda operates in exactly the opposite direction. The Jews pinned their hopes for integrating into modern society on promoting the moral sense. Homosexuals have pinned their integration into society on

promoting the aesthetic sense. Camp is a solvent of morality. It neutralizes moral indignation, sponsors playfulness.

53. Nevertheless, even though homosexuals have been its vanguard, Camp taste is much more than homosexual taste. Obviously, its metaphor of life as theater is peculiarly suited as a justification and projection of a certain aspect of the situation of homosexuals. (The Camp insistence on not being 'serious', on playing, also connects with the homosexual's desire to remain youthful.) Yet one feels that if homosexuals hadn't more or less invented Camp, someone else would. For the aristocratic posture with relation to culture cannot die, though it may persist only in increasingly arbitrary and ingenious ways. Camp is (to repeat) the relation to style in a time in which the adoption of style – as such – has become altogether questionable. (In the modern era, each new style, unless frankly anachronistic, has come on the scene as an anti-style.)

'One must have a heart of stone to read the death of Little Nell without laughing.'

– *In conversation*

54. The experiences of Camp are based on the great discovery that the sensibility of high culture has no monopoly upon refinement. Camp asserts that good taste is not simply good taste; that there exists, indeed, a good taste of bad taste. (Genet talks about this in *Our Lady of the Flowers*.) The discovery of the good taste of bad taste can be very liberating. The man who insists on high and serious pleasures is depriving himself of pleasure; he continually restricts what he can enjoy; in the constant exercise of his good taste he will eventually price himself out of the market, so to speak. Here Camp taste supervenes upon good taste as a daring and witty hedonism. It makes the man of good taste cheerful, where before he ran the risk of being chronically frustrated. It is good for the digestion.

55. Camp taste is, above all, a mode of enjoyment, of appreciation – not judgment. Camp is generous. It wants to enjoy. It only seems like malice, cynicism. (Or, if it is cynicism, it's not a ruthless but a sweet cynicism.) Camp taste doesn't propose that it is in bad taste to be serious; it doesn't sneer at someone who succeeds in being seriously dramatic. What it does is to find the success in certain passionate failures.

56. Camp taste is a kind of love, love for human nature. It relishes, rather than judges, the little triumphs and awkward intensities of 'character'. . . . Camp taste identifies with what it is enjoying. People who share this sensibility are not laughing at the thing they label as 'a camp', they're enjoying it. Camp is a *tender* feeling.

(Here, one may compare Camp with much of Pop Art, which – when it is not just Camp – embodies an attitude that is related, but still very different. Pop Art is more flat and more dry, more serious, more detached, ultimately nihilistic.)

57. Camp taste nourishes itself on the love that has gone into certain objects and personal styles. The absence of this love is the reason why such kitsch items as *Peyton Place* (the book) and the Tishman Building aren't Camp.

58. The ultimate Camp statement: it's good because it's awful . . . Of course, one can't always say that. Only under certain conditions, those which I've tried to sketch in these notes.

One Culture and the New Sensibility

In the last few years there has been a good deal of discussion of a purported chasm which opened up some two centuries ago, with the advent of the Industrial Revolution, between 'two cultures', the literary-artistic and the scientific. According to this diagnosis, any intelligent and articulate modern person is likely to inhabit one culture to the exclusion of the other. He will be concerned with different documents, different techniques, different problems; he will speak a different language. Most important, the type of effort required for the mastery of these two cultures will differ vastly. For the literary-artistic culture is understood as a general culture. It is addressed to man insofar as he is man; it is culture or, rather, it promotes culture, in the sense of culture defined by Ortega y Gasset: that which a man has in his possession when he has forgotten everything that he has read. The scientific culture, in contrast, is a culture for specialists; it is founded on remembering and is set down in ways that require complete dedication of the effort to comprehend. While the literary-artistic culture aims at internalization, ingestion – in other words, cultivation – the scientific culture aims at accumulation and externalization in complex instruments for problem-solving and specific techniques for mastery.

Though T. S. Eliot derived the chasm between the two cultures from a period more remote in modern history, speaking in a famous essay of a 'dissociation of sensibility' which opened up in the 17th century, the connection of the problem with the Industrial Revolution seems well taken. There is a historic antipathy on the part of many literary intellectuals and artists to those changes which characterize modern society – above all, industrialization and those of its effects which everyone has experienced, such as the proliferation of huge impersonal cities and the predominance of the anonymous style of urban life. It has mattered little whether industrialization, the creature of modern 'science', is seen on the 19th and early-20th-century model, as noisy smoky artificial processes which defile nature and standardize culture or on the newer model, the clean automated technology that is coming into being in the second half of the 20th century. The judgment has been mostly the same. Literary men, feeling that the status of humanity itself was being challenged by the new science and the new technology, abhorred and deplored the change. But the literary men, whether one thinks of Emerson and Thoreau and Ruskin in the 19th century, or of 20th-century intellectuals who talk of modern society as being in some new way incomprehensible, 'alienated', are inevitably on the defensive. They know that the scientific culture, the coming of the machine, cannot be stopped.

The standard response to the problem of 'the two cultures' – and the issue long antedates by many decades the crude and philistine statement of the problem by C. P. Snow in a famous lecture some years ago – has been a facile defense of the function of the arts (in terms of an ever vaguer ideology of 'humanism') or a premature surrender of the function of the arts to science. By the second response, I am not referring to the philistinism of scientists (and those of their party among artists and philosophers) who dismiss the arts as imprecise, untrue, at best mere toys. I am speaking of serious doubts which have arisen among those who are passionately engaged in the arts. The role of the individual artist, in the business of making unique objects for the purpose of giving pleasure and educating conscience and sensibility, has repeatedly been called into question. Some literary intellectuals and artists have gone so far as to prophesy the ultimate demise of the art-making activity of man. Art, in an automated scientific society, would be unfunctional, useless.

But this conclusion, I should argue, is plainly unwarranted. Indeed, the whole issue seems to me crudely put. For the question of 'the two cultures' assumes that science and technology are changing, in motion, while the arts are static, fulfilling some perennial generic human function (consolation? edification? diversion?). Only on the basis of this false assumption would anyone reason that the arts might be in danger of becoming obsolete.

Art does not progress, in the sense that science and technology do. But the arts do develop and change. For instance, in our own time, art is becoming increasingly the terrain of specialists. The most interesting and creative art of our time is *not* open to the generally educated; it demands special effort; it speaks a specialized language. The music of Milton Babbitt and Morton Feldman, the painting of Mark Rothko and Frank Stella, the dance of Merce Cunningham and James Waring demand an education of sensibility whose difficulties and length of apprenticeship are at least comparable to the difficulties of mastering physics or engineering. (Only the novel, among the arts, at least in America, fails to provide similar examples.) The parallel between the abstruseness of contemporary art and that of modern science is too obvious to be missed. Another likeness to the scientific culture is the history-mindedness of contemporary art. The most interesting works of contemporary art are full of references to the history of the medium; so far as they comment on past art, they demand a knowledge of at least the recent past. As Harold Rosenberg has pointed out, contemporary paintings are themselves acts of criticism as much as of creation. The point could be made as well of much recent work in the films, music, the dance, poetry, and (in Europe) literature. Again, a similarity with the style of science – this time, with the accumulative aspect of science – can be discerned.

The conflict between 'the two cultures' is in fact an illusion, a temporary phenomenon born of a period of profound and bewildering historical change. What we are witnessing is not so much a conflict of cultures as the creation of a new (potentially unitary) kind of sensibility. This new sensibility is rooted, as it must be, in our experience, experiences which are new in the history of humanity – in extreme social and physical mobility; in the crowdedness of the human scene (both people and material commodities multiplying at a dizzying rate); in the availability of new sensations such as speed (physical speed, as in airplane travel; speed of images, as in the cinema); and in the pan-cultural perspective on the arts that is possible through the mass reproduction of art objects.

What we are getting is not the demise of art, but a transformation of the function of art. Art, which arose in human society as a magical-religious operation, and passed over into a technique for depicting and commenting on secular reality, has in our own time arrogated to itself a new function – neither

religious, nor serving a secularized religious function, nor merely secular or profane (a notion which
breaks down when its opposite, the 'religious' or
'sacred', becomes obsolescent). Art today is a new
kind of instrument, an instrument for modifying
consciousness and organizing new modes of sensibility. And the means for practicing art have been
radically extended. Indeed, in response to this new
function (more felt than clearly articulated), artists
have had to become self-conscious aestheticians:
continually challenging their means, their materials
and methods. Often, the conquest and exploitation
of new materials and methods drawn from the world
of 'non-art' – for example, from industrial technology, from commercial processes and imagery, from
purely private and subjective fantasies and dreams –
seems to be the principal effort of many artists.
Painters no longer feel themselves confined to canvas
and paint, but employ hair, photographs, wax, sand,
bicycle tires, their own toothbrushes and socks.
Musicians have reached beyond the sounds of the
traditional instruments to use tampered instruments
and (usually on tape) synthetic sounds and industrial noises.

All kinds of conventionally accepted boundaries have thereby been challenged: not just the one between the 'scientific' and the 'literary-artistic' cultures, or the one between 'art' and 'non-art'; but also many established distinctions within the world of culture itself – that between form and content, the frivolous and the serious, and (a favorite of literary intellectuals) 'high' and 'low' culture.

The distinction between 'high' and 'low' (or 'mass' or 'popular') culture is based partly on an evaluation of the difference between unique and mass-produced objects. In an era of mass technological reproduction, the work of the serious artist had a special value simply because it was unique, because it bore his personal, individual signature. The works of popular culture (and even films were for a long time included in this category) were seen as having little value because they were manufactured objects, bearing no individual stamp – group concoctions made for an undifferentiated audience. But in the light of contemporary practice in the arts, this distinction appears extremely shallow. Many of the serious works of art of recent decades have a decidedly impersonal character. The work of art is reasserting its existence as 'object' (even as manufactured or mass-produced object, drawing on the popular arts) rather than as 'individual personal expression'.

The exploration of the impersonal (and transpersonal) in contemporary art is the new classicism; at least, a reaction against what is understood as the romantic spirit dominates most of the interesting art of today. Today's art, with its insistence on coolness, its refusal of what it considers to be sentimentality, its spirit of exactness, its sense of 'research' and 'problems', is closer to the spirit of science than of art in the old-fashioned sense. Often, the artist's work is only his idea, his concept. This is a familiar practice in architecture, of course. And one remembers that painters in the Renaissance often left parts of their canvases to be worked out by students, and that in the flourishing period of the concerto the cadenza at the end of the first movement was left to the inventiveness and discretion of the performing soloist. But similar practices have a different, more polemical meaning today, in the present post-romantic era of the arts. When painters such as Joseph Albers, Ellsworth Kelly and Andy Warhol assign portions of the work, say, the painting in of the colors themselves, to a friend or the local gardener; when musicians such as Stockhausen, John Cage and Luigi Nono invite collaboration from performers by leaving opportunities for random effects, switching around the order of the score, and improvisations – they are changing the ground rules which most of us employ to recognize a work of art. They are saying what art need not be. At least, not necessarily.

The primary feature of the new sensibility is that its model product is not the literary work, above all, the novel. A new non-literary culture exists today, of whose very existence, not to mention significance, most literary intellectuals are entirely unaware. This new establishment includes certain painters, sculptors, architects, social planners, film-makers, TV technicians, neurologists, musicians, electronics engineers, dancers, philosophers and sociologists. (A few poets and prose writers can be included.) Some of the basic texts for this new cultural alignment are to be found in the writings of Nietzsche, Wittgenstein, Antonin Artaud, C. S. Sherrington, Buckminster Fuller, Marshall McLuhan, John Cage, André Breton,

Roland Barthes, Claude Lévi-Strauss, Sigfried Giedon, Norman O. Brown, and György Kepes.

Those who worry about the gap between 'the two cultures', and this means virtually all literary intellectuals in England and America, take for granted a notion of culture which decidedly needs re-examining. It is the notion perhaps best expressed by Matthew Arnold (in which the central cultural act is the making of literature, which is itself understood as the criticism of culture). Simply ignorant of the vital and enthralling (so called 'avant-garde') developments in the other arts, and blinded by their personal investment in the perpetuation of the older notion of culture, they continue to cling to literature as the model for creative statement.

What gives literature its pre-eminence is its heavy burden of 'content', both reportage and moral judgment. (This makes it possible for most English and American literary critics to use literary works mainly as texts, or even pretexts, for social and cultural diagnosis – rather than concentrating on the properties of, say, a given novel or a play, as an art work.) But the model arts of our time are actually those with much less content, and a much cooler mode of moral judgment – like music, films, dance, architecture, painting, sculpture. The practice of these arts – all of which draw profusely, naturally, and without embarrassment, upon science and technology – are the locus of the new sensibility.

The problem of 'the two cultures', in short, rests upon an uneducated, uncontemporary grasp of our present cultural situation. It arises from the ignorance of literary intellectuals (and of scientists with a shallow knowledge of the arts, like the scientist-novelist C. P. Snow himself) of a new culture, and its emerging sensibility. In fact, there can be no divorce between science and technology, on the one hand, and art, on the other, any more than there can be a divorce between art and the forms of social life. Works of art, psychological forms, and social forms all reflect each other, and change with each other. But, of course, most people are slow to come to terms with such changes – especially today, when the changes are occurring with an unprecedented rapidity. Marshall McLuhan has described human history as a succession of acts of technological extension of human capacity, each of which works a radical change upon our environment and our ways of thinking, feeling and valuing. The tendency, he remarks, is to upgrade the old environment into art form (thus Nature became a vessel of aesthetic and spiritual values in the new industrial environment) 'while the new conditions are regarded as corrupt and degrading.' Typically, it is only certain artists in any given era who 'have the resources and temerity to live in immediate contact with the environment of their age . . . That is why they may seem to be "ahead of their time" . . . More timid people prefer to accept the . . . previous environment's values as the continuing reality of their time. Our natural bias is to accept the new gimmick (automation, say) as a thing that can be accommodated in the old ethical order.' Only in the terms of what McLuhan calls the old ethical order does the problem of 'the two cultures' appear to be a genuine problem. It is not a problem for most of the creative artists of our time (among whom one could include very few novelists) because most of these artists have broken, whether they know it or not, with the Matthew Arnold notion of culture, finding it historically and humanly obsolescent.

The Matthew Arnold notion of culture defines art as the criticism of life – this being understood as the propounding of moral, social and political ideas. The new sensibility understands art as the extension of life – this being understood as the representation of (new) modes of vivacity. There is no necessary denial of the role of moral evaluation here. Only the scale has changed; it has become less gross, and what it sacrifices in discursive explicitness it gains in accuracy and subliminal power. For we are what we are able to see (hear, taste, smell, feel) even more powerfully and profoundly than we are what furniture of ideas we have stocked in our heads. Of course, the proponents of 'the two cultures' crisis continue to observe a desperate contrast between unintelligible, morally neutral science and technology, on the one hand, and morally committed, human-scale art on the other. But matters are not that simple, and never were. A great work of art is never simply (or even mainly) a vehicle of ideas or of moral sentiments. It is, first of all, an object modifying our consciousness and sensibility, changing the composition, however slightly, of the humus that nourishes all specific ideas and sentiments. Outraged humanists, please note.

There is no need for alarm. A work of art does not cease being a moment in the conscience of mankind, when moral conscience is understood as only one of the functions of consciousness.

Sensations, feelings, the abstract forms and styles of sensibility count. It is to these that contemporary art addresses itself. The basic unit for contemporary art is not the idea, but the analysis of and extension of sensations. (Or if it is an 'idea', it is about the form of sensibility.) Rilke described the artist as someone who works 'toward an extension of the regions of the individual senses'; McLuhan calls artists 'experts in sensory awareness'. And the most interesting works of contemporary art (one can begin at least as far back as French symbolist poetry) are adventures in sensation, new 'sensory mixes'. Such art is, in principle, experimental – not out of an elitist disdain for what is accessible to the majority, but precisely in the sense that science is experimental. Such an art is also notably apolitical and undidactic, or, rather, infra-didactic.

When Ortega y Gasset wrote his famous essay *The Dehumanization of Art* in the early 1920s, he ascribed the qualities of modern art (such as impersonality, the ban on pathos, hostility to the past, playfulness, willful stylization, absence of ethical and political commitment) to the spirit of youth which he thought dominated our age.* In retrospect, it seems this 'dehumanization' did not signify the recovery of childlike innocence, but was rather a very adult, knowing response. What other response than anguish, followed by anesthesia and then by wit and the elevating of intelligence over sentiment, is possible as a response to the social disorder and mass atrocities of our time, and – equally important for our sensibilities, but less often remarked on – to the unprecedented change in what rules our environment from the intelligible and visible to that which is only with difficulty intelligible, and is invisible? Art, which I have characterized as an instrument for modifying and educating sensibility and consciousness, now operates in an environment which cannot be grasped by the senses.

* Ortega remarks, in this essay: 'Were art to redeem man, it could do so only by saving him from the seriousness of life and restoring him to an unexpected boyishness.'

Susan Sontag

Buckminister Fuller has written:

> In World War I industry suddenly went from the
> visible to the invisible base, from the track to the
> trackless, from the wire to the wireless, from
> visible structuring to invisible structuring in
> alloys. The big thing about World War I is that
> man went off the sensorial spectrum forever as
> the prime criterion of accrediting innova-
> tions . . . All major advances since World War I
> have been in the infra- and the ultrasensorial
> frequencies of the electromagnetic spectrum.
> All the important technical affairs of men
> today are invisible . . . The old masters, who
> were sensorialists, have unleased a Pandora's
> box of non-sensorially controllable phenomena,
> which they had avoided accrediting up to that
> time . . . Suddenly they lost their true mastery,
> because from then on they didn't personally
> understand what was going on. If you don't
> understand you cannot master . . . Since World
> War I, the old masters have been extinct . . .

But, of course, art remains permanently tied to the
senses. Just as one cannot float colors in space (a

painter needs some sort of surface, like a canvas, however neutral and textureless), one cannot have a work of art that does not impinge upon the human sensorium. But it is important to realize that human sensory awareness has not merely a biology but a specific history, each culture placing a premium on certain senses and inhibiting others. (The same is true for the range of primary human emotions.) Here is where art (among other things) enters, and why the interesting art of our time has such a feeling of anguish and crisis about it, however playful and abstract and ostensibly neutral morally it may appear. Western man may be said to have been undergoing a massive sensory anesthesia (a concomitant of the process that Max Weber calls 'bureaucratic rationalization') at least since the Industrial Revolution, with modern art functioning as a kind of shock therapy for both confounding and unclosing our senses.

One important consequence of the new sensibility (with its abandonment of the Matthew Arnold idea of culture) has already been alluded to – namely, that the distinction between 'high' and 'low' culture seems less and less meaningful. For such a distinction – inseparable from the Matthew Arnold apparatus – simply does not make sense for a creative community of artists and scientists engaged in programming sensations, uninterested in art as a species of moral journalism. Art has always been more than that, anyway.

Another way of characterizing the present cultural situation, in its most creative aspects, would be to speak of a new attitude toward pleasure. In one sense, the new art and the new sensibility take a rather dim view of pleasure. (The great contemporary French composer, Pierre Boulez, entitled an important essay of his twelve years ago, 'Against Hedonism in Music'.) The seriousness of modern art precludes pleasure in the familiar sense – the pleasure of a melody that one can hum after leaving the concert hall, of characters in a novel or play whom one can recognize, identify with, and dissect in terms of realistic psychological motives, of a beautiful landscape or a dramatic moment represented on a canvas. If hedonism means sustaining the old ways in which we have found pleasure in art (the old sensory and psychic modalities), then the new art is anti-hedonistic. Having one's sensorium challenged or stretched hurts. The new serious music hurts one's ears, the new painting does not graciously reward one's sight, the new films and the few interesting new prose works do not go down easily. The commonest complaint about the films of Antonioni or the narratives of Beckett or Burroughs is that they are hard to look at or to read, that they are 'boring.' But the charge of boredom is really hypocritical. There is, in a sense, no such thing as boredom. Boredom is only another name for a certain species of frustration. And the new languages which the interesting art of our time speaks are frustrating to the sensibilities of most educated people.

But the purpose of art is always, ultimately, to give pleasure – though our sensibilities may take time to catch up with the forms of pleasure that art in a given time may offer. And, one can also say that, balancing the ostensible anti-hedonism of serious contemporary art, the modern sensibility is more involved with pleasure in the familiar sense than ever. Because the new sensibility demands less 'content' in art, and is more open to the pleasures of 'form' and style, it is also less snobbish, less moralistic – in that it does not demand that pleasure in art necessarily be associated with edification. If art is understood as a form of discipline of the feelings and a programming of sensations, then the feeling (or sensation) given off by a Rauschenberg painting might be like that of a song by the Supremes. The brio and elegance of Budd Boetticher's *The Rise and Fall of Legs Diamond* or the singing style of Dionne Warwick can be appreciated as a complex and pleasurable event. They are experienced without condescension.

This last point seems to me worth underscoring. For it is important to understand that the affection which many younger artists and intellectuals feel for the popular arts is not a new philistinism (as has so often been charged) or a species of anti-intellectualism or some kind of abdication from culture. The fact that many of the most serious American painters, for example, are also fans of 'the new sound' in popular music is *not* the result of the search for mere diversion or relaxation; it is not, say, like Schoenberg also playing tennis. It reflects a new, more open way of looking at the world and at things in the world, our world. It does not mean the renunciation of all standards: there is plenty of stupid popular music, as well as inferior and pretentious 'avant-garde' paintings, films, and music. The point is that there are new standards, new standards of beauty and style and taste. The new sensibility is defiantly pluralistic; it is dedicated both to an excruciating seriousness and to fun and wit and nostalgia. It is also extremely history-conscious; and the voracity of its enthusiasms (and of the supercession of these enthusiasms) is very high-speed and hectic. From the vantage point of this new sensibility, the beauty of a machine or of the solution to a mathematical problem, of a painting by Jasper Johns, of a film by Jean-Luc Godard, and of the personalities and music of the Beatles is equally accessible.